This edition published by Parragon Books Ltd in 2014

Parragon Books Ltd
Chartist House
15–17 Trim Street
Bath BA1 1HA, UK
www.parragon.com

ISBN 978-1-4723-3769-6

Printed in China

nickelodeon™

TEENAGE MUTANT NINJA TURTLES™

GREEN TEAM!

Parragon

Bath • New York • Singapore • Hong Kong • Cologne • Delhi
Melbourne • Amsterdam • Johannesburg • Shenzhen

A long time ago, a man named Hamato Yoshi bought four turtles at a pet store. As he left, he passed a man on the street who was walking in a strange way, almost like a robot. Hamato decided to follow him.

In an alleyway, a rat ran up Hamato's leg. The strange man saw Hamato and threw a canister at him – **SMASH!** The canister broke, splashing green goo all over Hamato, the turtles and the rat. The goo caused a chemical reaction! The turtles grew to human size and Hamato grew fur and a tail. He became a human rat!

That day, Hamato and the turtles became mutants.

Hamato Yoshi became Splinter. For fifteen years, he and the Turtles all lived together in the sewer. The Turtles called Splinter 'Sensei', which means 'teacher'. He was teaching the Turtles how to be ninjas. They were the Teenage Mutant Ninja Turtles!

Leonardo was brave.

Michelangelo liked to have fun.

Donatello was smart and loved gadgets.

Raphael was tough.

On their fifteenth birthday, the Turtles wanted to see the City. The Turtles had never been above ground. Splinter thought that people would be afraid of them.

"Do you think we're ready, Sensei?" Leonardo asked.

"Yes and no," Splinter replied. In the end, he let them go. "Don't let anyone see you," he warned.

The Turtles cheered.

The Turtles peeked out of a manhole and saw the street for the first time. It was dark and spooky. There was dirt and rubbish everywhere....

"It's so beautiful," Michelangelo said.

The city was filled with incredible surprises. The best one was ... pizza!

"I never thought I'd taste anything better than worms and algae," said Raphael. "This is amazing!"

"It's great up here!" said Michelangelo.

As the Turtles headed back to the sewer, they saw a girl walking with her dad. Her name was April.

"She's the most beautiful girl I've ever seen," Donatello said.

"She's the only girl you've ever seen!" Raphael replied.

Suddenly a van screeched to a stop. Strangers jumped out and grabbed April and her dad!

The Turtles rushed to help, but they kept bumping into each other. Leonardo hit Raphael and Michelangelo tripped over Donatello. While the Turtles were tangled up, the strangers escaped with April and her dad.

One bad guy was left behind. After Michelangelo had won the fight with him, something strange happened. **BLOOP!** A weird pink blob popped out of the bad guy's chest – he was really a robot with a brain!

The brain scurried away before Michelangelo could show anyone. When he told his brothers about it, they didn't believe him.

Back in the sewer, the Turtles told Splinter about the failed rescue attempt.

"I need to train you as a team," Splinter said. "Next year you can go to the surface again."

But Donatello couldn't wait. He wanted to save April straight away!

Splinter nodded. "Then you will need a leader." He chose Leonardo.

The next night, the Turtles returned to the streets and tracked down the van that the bad guys had used. The Turtles hid and waited for the driver to come back.

When he saw the driver coming, Leonardo said, "I have a daring plan." But the other Turtles were already running towards the van!

The Turtles chased after the van as it drove away. They jumped over rooftops to keep up. Leonardo threw a Throwing Star weapon and punctured the van's tyre! It swerved and crashed.

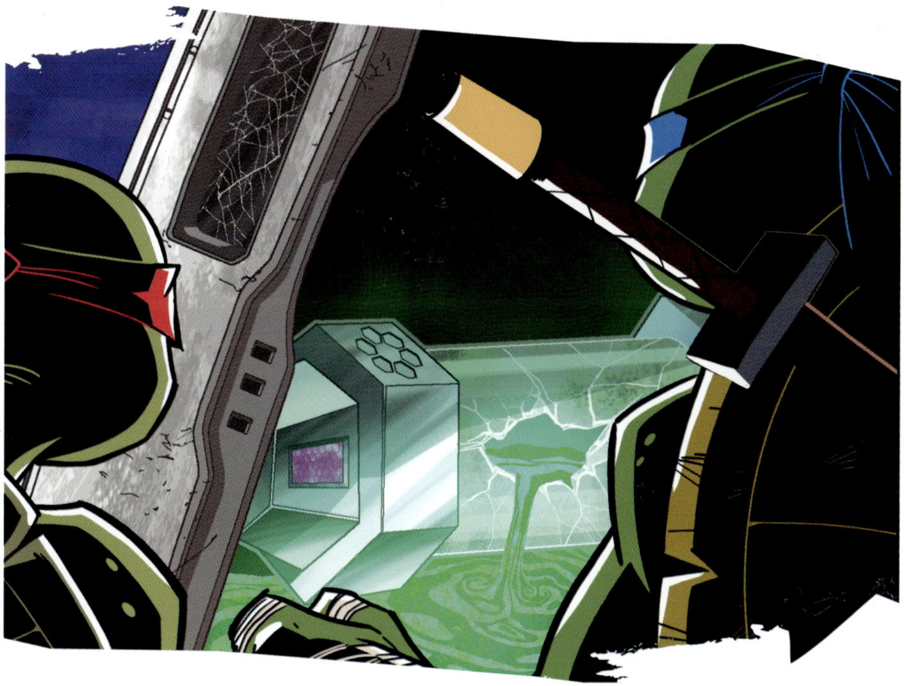

Raphael opened the back of the van. It was full of the same green goo that had turned the Turtles into mutants!

"This is huge," Leonardo said. "These bad guys have something to do with us."

"How is that possible?" Donatello asked.

"Anything is possible for alien robots!" Michelangelo said.

Raphael took a canister of green goo from the van and shoved it in the driver's face.

"This stuff can turn you into a mutant like us," he said. "Tell us what's going on." He tipped the canister a bit.

"Okay!" the driver said. "My name is Snake. Those guys are called the Kraang. They're grabbing scientists. I don't know why."

Snake showed the Turtles the Kraang's hideout.

Raphael wanted to attack right away, but Leonardo wanted to make a plan first. While they were arguing, Snake escaped!

The Turtles chased Snake over the rooftops and into an alleyway. But he disappeared! Leonardo spotted Snake hiding behind some bins and nudged Raphael. Leonardo had a plan.

"Oh great, we let him get away," Leonardo said loudly so that Snake could hear him. "Let's drive the van up to the gate at midnight."

Later, the van raced up to the door of the Kraang's hideout. Snake and the Kraang thought it was the Turtles. **ZAP!** They destroyed the van! Green goo splashed everywhere and covered Snake. But the van was empty. Where were the Turtles?

The Turtles had created the distraction so that they could sneak into the hideout! They discovered that the Kraang were really brain-like aliens that used robots to move around. They wanted April's dad, a famous scientist, to help them with an evil plan.

The Turtles searched the hideout for April and her dad. They found a holding cell – April and her dad were inside! Donatello tried to pick the lock but it wouldn't open.

Raphael started smashing the door! Just as it was about to break, the Kraang came back and dragged April and her dad away.

The Turtles started to chase the Kraang, but Snake blocked their path. Now Snake was huge! He was covered in leaves and thorns. The green goo had mutated him!

"It's Snake, but he's a giant weed!" Leonardo said.

"He's Snakeweed!" Michelangelo said.

The Turtles tried to fight past Snakeweed. But every time they sliced off one of his branches, it grew straight back.

"No fair!" Donatello said.

Some of the Kraang forced April and her dad into a helicopter. As it took off, Donatello leaped onto one of its landing skids to stop them. The helicopter spun and rocked and April fell out!

Donatello saved April, but the Kraang flew away with her dad.

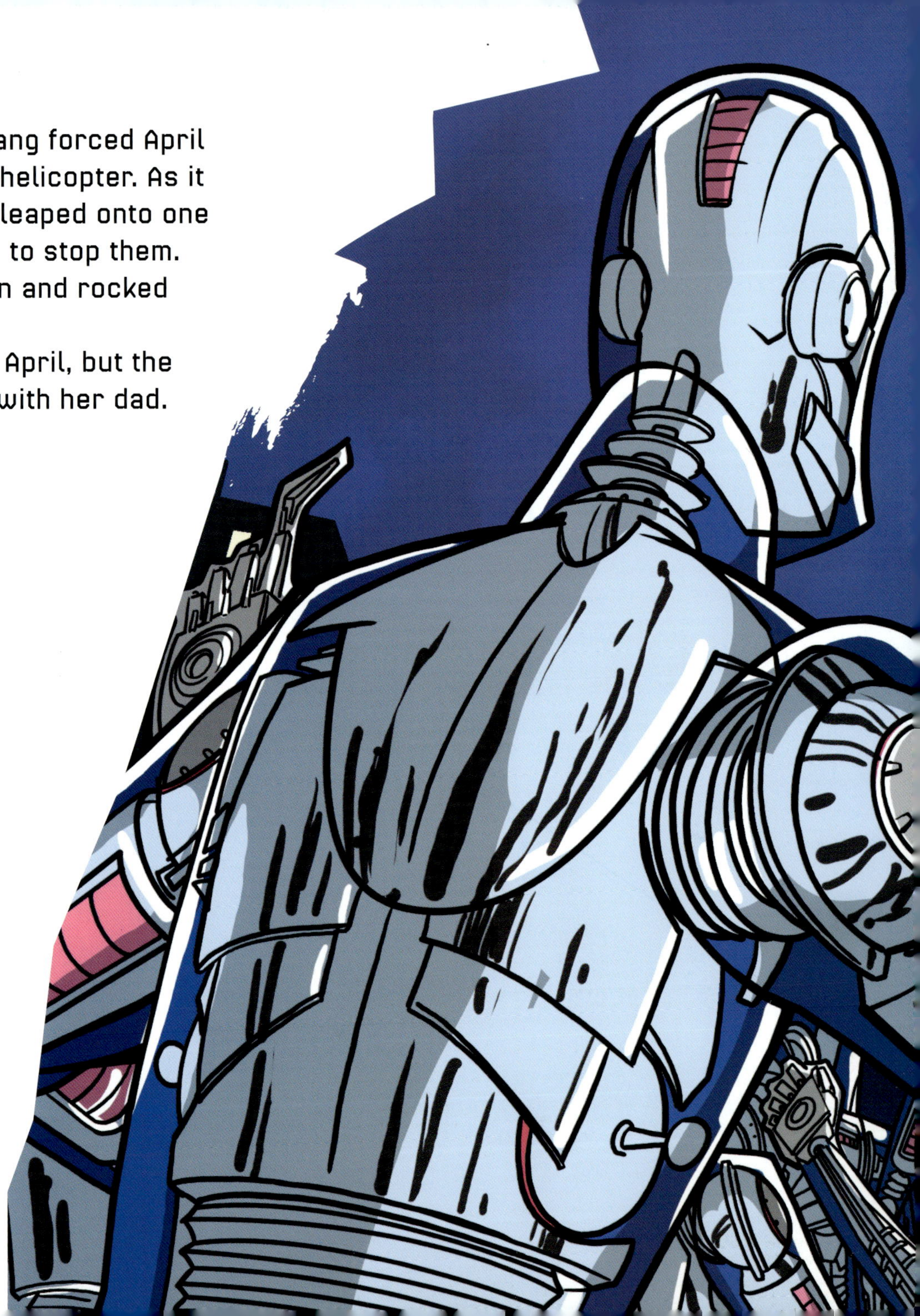

The rest of the Kraang turned back towards the Turtles, who were now stuck between Snakeweed and the Kraang!

Suddenly, Leonardo had an idea. He ran to the hideout's power generator. The Kraang turned their blasters towards him and fired, but Leonardo jumped aside at the last second.

KABLAAM! The Kraang's blasters blew up the generator and destroyed the hideout! The Turtles and April tumbled away from the blast.

The Turtles accompanied April back home. She was safe, but the Kraang still had her father.

"We won't rest until we find him," Donatello said.

"We?" asked April. "This isn't your fight."

"It is now," said Donatello. "Because we are a team!"